PRESIDENTS

RICHARD M. NIXON

A MyReportLinks.com Book

Randy Schultz

MyReportLinks.com Books

an imprint of

Enslow Publishers, Inc.

Box 398, 40 Industrial Road
Berkeley Heights, NJ 07922
USA

MyReportLinks.com Books, an imprint of Enslow Publishers, Inc. MyReportLinks is a trademark of Enslow Publishers, Inc.

Library of Congress Cataloging-in-Publication Data

Schultz, Randy.
  Richard M. Nixon / Randy Schultz.
    p. cm. — (Presidents)
Summary: A biography of the thirty-seventh president of the United States, describing his personal life and political career, including the Watergate scandal. Includes Internet links to Web sites, source documents, and photographs related to Richard Nixon.
Includes bibliographical references and index.
  ISBN 0-7660-5104-8
  1. Nixon, Richard M. (Richard Milhous), 1913—-Juvenile literature.
  2. Presidents—United States—Biography—Juvenile literature. [1. Nixon, Richard M. (Richard Milhous), 1913- 2. Presidents.] I. Title.
II. Series.
E856.S288 2002
973.924'092—dc21

                                    2002014701

Printed in the United States of America

10 9 8 7 6 5 4 3 2 1

To Our Readers:
Through the purchase of this book, you and your library gain access to the Report Links that specifically back up this book.

The Publisher will provide access to the Report Links that back up this book and will keep these Report Links up to date on **www.myreportlinks.com** for three years from the book's first publication date.

We have done our best to make sure all Internet addresses in this book were active and appropriate when we went to press. However, the author and the Publisher have no control over, and assume no liability for, the material available on those Internet sites or on other Web sites they may link to.

The usage of the MyReportLinks.com Books Web site is subject to the terms and conditions stated on the Usage Policy Statement on **www.myreportlinks.com**.

In the future, a password may be required to access the Report Links that back up this book. The password is found on the bottom of page 4 of this book.

Any comments or suggestions can be sent by e-mail to comments@myreportlinks.com or to the address on the back cover.

Photo Credits: © Corel Corporation, pp. 1 (background), 3; © 1996–2003 The Washington Post Company, pp. 13, 15; © watergate.info 1995–2002, p. 11; Courtesy Dwight D. Eisenhower Library/National Park Service, p. 28; Department of the Interior, p. 34; Dwight D. Eisenhower Library, p. 26; Enslow Publishers, Inc., p. 44; MyReportLinks.com Books, p. 4; National Archives and Records Administration, pp. 36, 41; National Park Service, p. 29; National Space Science Data Center, p. 38; Nixon Presidential Materials Project, p. 17; Richard Nixon Library & Birthplace, pp. 1, 19, 21, 24, 31, 43; PBS, p. 33; Whittier College, p. 18.

Cover Photo: © Corel Corporation (background); Richard Nixon Library & Birthplace (portrait).

Contents

About MyReportLinks.com Books

MyReportLinks.com Books
Great Books, Great Links, Great for Research!

MyReportLinks.com Books present the information you need to learn about your report subject. In addition, they show you where to go on the Internet for more information. The pre-evaluated Report Links that back up this book are kept up to date on **www.myreportlinks.com**. With the purchase of a MyReportLinks.com Books title, you and your library gain access to the Report Links that specifically back up that book. The Report Links save hours of research time and link to dozens—even hundreds—of Web sites, source documents, and photos related to your report topic.

Please see "To Our Readers" on the Copyright page for important information about this book, the MyReportLinks.com Books Web site, and the Report Links that back up this book.

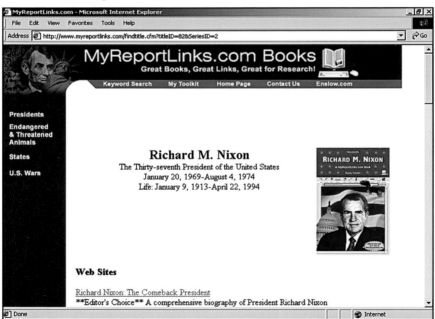

Access:

The Publisher will provide access to the Report Links that back up this book and will try to keep these Report Links up to date on our Web site for three years from the book's first publication date. Please enter **PNI9845** if asked for a password.

Report Links

 The Internet sites described below can be accessed at
http://www.myreportlinks.com

*EDITOR'S CHOICE

▶ **Richard Nixon: The Comeback President**
At this Web site you will find a comprehensive biography of Richard
Nixon where you will learn about his early life, domestic and foreign
affairs, the first lady, and much more.

Link to this Internet site from http://www.myreportlinks.com

*EDITOR'S CHOICE

▶ **The American Experience: Nixon's China Game**
Within this site you will find an essay about Nixon's trip to China,
transcripts of interviews with American and Chinese participants, and
an interactive time line of United States relations with China.

Link to this Internet site from http://www.myreportlinks.com

*EDITOR'S CHOICE

▶ **washingtonpost.com: Revisiting Watergate**
Washington Post.com revisits the Watergate scandal through past
articles, a chronology of events, documents, and brief profiles of the
key players. You can also take an interactive quiz!

Link to this Internet site from http://www.myreportlinks.com

*EDITOR'S CHOICE

▶ **CNN: Cold War**
CNN provides a comprehensive look at the Cold War. Here you will
learn about Cold War culture, technology, espionage, and the atomic
bomb. You will also find profiles of key players, historical documents,
interactive maps, and much more.

Link to this Internet site from http://www.myreportlinks.com

*EDITOR'S CHOICE

▶ **The American Experience: Vietnam Online**
Here you will find a history of the Vietnam War from its origins in
1945 up until 1997. Biographies of key players, an interactive time
line, personal accounts of participants, and other resources are available.

Link to this Internet site from http://www.myreportlinks.com

*EDITOR'S CHOICE

▶ **American Presidents: Life Portraits: Richard M. Nixon**
At this Web site you will find "Life Facts" and "Did you know?" trivia
about Richard M. Nixon. You will also find a letter written by Nixon
to the parents of a soldier who died in the Vietnam War.

Link to this Internet site from http://www.myreportlinks.com

 The Internet sites described below can be accessed at
http://www.myreportlinks.com

▶ **The Alger Hiss Case**
This article provides an in-depth look at the two Alger Hiss trials. Here you
will find biographical information about those involved, recent developments
related to the case, and an extensive bibliography.

Link to this Internet site from http://www.myreportlinks.com

▶ **The American Presidency: Richard M. Nixon**
This Web site includes an in-depth biography of Richard M. Nixon. Here you
will learn about his life, career in Congress, vice presidency, and presidency.
You will also learn about Watergate and Nixon's resignation.

Link to this Internet site from http://www.myreportlinks.com

▶ **The American Presidency: Spiro T. Agnew**
At this Web site you will find the biography of Vice President Spiro T. Agnew.
Learn about Agnew's vice presidency and eventual resignation.

Link to this Internet site from http://www.myreportlinks.com

▶ *Apollo 11*
Visit NASA's home page to learn about the *Apollo 11* mission. Here you can
learn the history of the mission, listen to audio clips, and view photographs of
one of the most important events in American history.

Link to this Internet site from http://www.myreportlinks.com

▶ **CNN: AllPolitics: President Richard Nixon's Resignation Speech**
Here you can read, or listen to, the complete text of Richard Nixon's 1974
resignation speech. Navigate using the links on the left to learn more about
the Watergate scandal.

Link to this Internet site from http://www.myreportlinks.com

▶ **c-span.org: Nixon White House Phone Calls**
Here you will find excerpts from recorded conversations between President
Nixon and his staff or between him and visitors. A history of the "Nixon
White House Tapes" is also included.

Link to this Internet site from http://www.myreportlinks.com

Report Links

▶**Debate History: 1960 Debates**

The complete text of four televised debates from the 1960 presidential election between John F. Kennedy and Richard M. Nixon.

Link to this Internet site from http://www.myreportlinks.com

▶**FAS: Space Policy Project: Safeguard**

At the online home of the Federation of American Scientists, you will find an in-depth article about Safeguard, the antiballistic missile (ABM) system proposed by the Nixon administration.

Link to this Internet site from http://www.myreportlinks.com

▶**Gerald Ford: The Accidental President**

At this Web site you will find a comprehensive biography of Gerald Ford. Here you will learn about his early life, vice presidency, presidency, and much more.

Link to this Internet site from http://www.myreportlinks.com

▶**The Great Debates of Nixon and Kennedy**

America's Story from America's Library, a Library of Congress Web site, tells the story of the debates between Richard Nixon and John F. Kennedy.

Link to this Internet site from http://www.myreportlinks.com

▶**Henry A. Kissinger—Biography**

By navigating through the Nobel eMuseum Web site you will find the biographies of Henry Kissinger and Le Duc Tho, as well as the 1973 Nobel Prize presentation speech. Here you will learn how Henry Kissinger and Le Duc Tho negotiated an end to the Vietnam War.

Link to this Internet site from http://www.myreportlinks.com

▶**The National Archives: When Nixon Met Elvis**

Here you will find the story and photographs of the Oval Office meeting between Elvis Presley and Richard Nixon. This meeting resulted in Presley's certification as an officer of the Bureau of Narcotics and Dangerous Drugs.

Link to this Internet site from http://www.myreportlinks.com

Report Links

The Internet sites described below can be accessed at http://www.myreportlinks.com

▶ *New York Times* **Obituary: The 37th President; In Three Decades**

Read the *New York Times* obituary of Richard M. Nixon. This obituary provides a comprehensive overview of Nixon's birth to the end of his first term in office.

Link to this Internet site from http://www.myreportlinks.com

▶ **Objects from the Presidency**

By navigating through this Web site you will find objects related to all United States presidents. You will also learn about the era of Nixon's administration and the office of the presidency.

Link to this Internet site from http://www.myreportlinks.com

▶ **Photographing History: Fred J. Maroon and the Nixon Years**

The National Museum of American History exhibits Fred J. Maroon's pictures from the last four years of Nixon's presidency. Featured are photographs from the White House, Nixon's reelection, the Watergate hearings, and his final days.

Link to this Internet site from http://www.myreportlinks.com

▶ **Richard Milhous Nixon**

At this Web site you will find facts and figures on Richard Nixon, including election results, a list of his cabinet members, notable events in his administration, historic documents, and more.

Link to this Internet site from http://www.myreportlinks.com

▶ **The Richard Nixon Library and Birthplace**

At the Richard Nixon Library and Birthplace you can take a virtual tour of the museum and visit the "Research Center" to find the biographies of Mr. and Mrs. Nixon, a bibliography of the Vietnam War, and speeches.

Link to this Internet site from http://www.myreportlinks.com

▶ **Senator Richard Nixon's "Checkers" Speech**

Here you will find the complete text of the first televised Richard Nixon speech. In this famous speech, Nixon defends himself against scandalous allegations.

Link to this Internet site from http://www.myreportlinks.com

Any comments? Contact us: **comments@myreportlinks.com**

Report Links

The Internet sites described below can be accessed at
http://www.myreportlinks.com

▶ **U.S. Environmental Protection Agency: History:
The Guardian: Origins of the EPA**
This page tells the story of the American ecological movement. Nixon
took the measure of passing the National Environmental Policy Act,
which created the Environmental Protection Agency.

Link to this Internet site from http://www.myreportlinks.com

▶ **The Wars for Vietnam: 1945–1975**
This Vietnam War site, from Vassar College, provides a comprehensive
overview of the war and holds a collection of related documents,
including the text of the Paris Accords, Nixon's "Vietnamization"
speech, and more.

Link to this Internet site from http://www.myreportlinks.com

▶ **watergate.info**
This Web sites meticulously covers the Watergate scandal. Here you
will find tape transcriptions, speeches, letters, and documents. You
will also find historical and biographical information about Nixon
and Ford.

Link to this Internet site from http://www.myreportlinks.com

▶ **The White House: Patricia Ryan Nixon**
The official White House Web site holds the biography of Patricia
Ryan Nixon. Here you will learn about her volunteer activities and
the diversity of arts and entertainment that she brought into the
White House.

Link to this Internet site from http://www.myreportlinks.com

▶ **The White House: Richard M. Nixon**
The official White House Web site holds the biography of Richard
Nixon. Here you will learn about the challenges he faced during
his administration.

Link to this Internet site from http://www.myreportlinks.com

▶ *World Almanac for Kids Online:* **Richard Milhous Nixon**
The *World Almanac for Kids Online* provides essential information
about Nixon, his vice presidency, presidency, Watergate, and
his resignation.

Link to this Internet site from http://www.myreportlinks.com

Highlights

1913—*Jan. 9:* Born in Yorba Linda, California, to Francis Anthony Nixon and Hannah Milhous Nixon.

1934—*June 9:* Graduates from Whittier College.

1937—*June 7:* Graduates from Duke University Law School.

1940—*June 21:* Marries Thelma Catherine (Patricia) Ryan, who becomes commonly referred to as Pat Nixon.

1943–1945—Serves as a naval officer during World War II.

1946—*Feb. 21:* Daughter, Patricia Nixon is born.

1948—*July 5:* Daughter, Julie Nixon is born.

1968—*Aug. 5–8:* Nominated for president at Republican National Convention. Spiro Agnew is nominated for vice president.

—*Nov. 5:* Defeats Hubert H. Humphrey to become the thirty-seventh president.

1969—*July 20:* First men land on the moon.

1970—*May 1:* Four students are killed by National Guardsmen during an antiwar demonstration at Kent State University in Ohio.

1971—*April 7:* Announces withdrawal of 100,000 U.S. soldiers from South Vietnam.

—*May 2–5:* Antiwar protests in Washington, D.C.

—*June 10:* Embargo on trade with Communist China is lifted.

1972—*May 26:* Signs U.S.-Soviet SALT I treaty.

—*June 17:* Five men are arrested in burglary of the Democratic National Committee headquarters in the Watergate building.

—*Nov. 7:* Wins reelection by defeating George McGovern.

1973—*Oct. 10:* Vice President Spiro Agnew resigns.

—*Dec. 6:* Gerald R. Ford is sworn in as vice president.

1974—*May 9:* House Judiciary Committee opens impeachment hearings.

—*Aug. 5:* White House transcripts are released, revealing that the president had directed the FBI to end the investigation of the Watergate break-in.

—*Aug. 9:* Nixon resigns; Ford becomes the thirty-eighth president.

1994—*April 22:* Nixon dies in New York City.

Chapter 1 ▶

The Watergate Scandal, 1973–1974

Watergate. To most people living in and around the Washington, D.C., area prior to 1973, the name Watergate meant nothing more than an office-hotel building complex located in the area.

By 1973, Watergate became known nationwide as a name for a scandal connected with President Richard

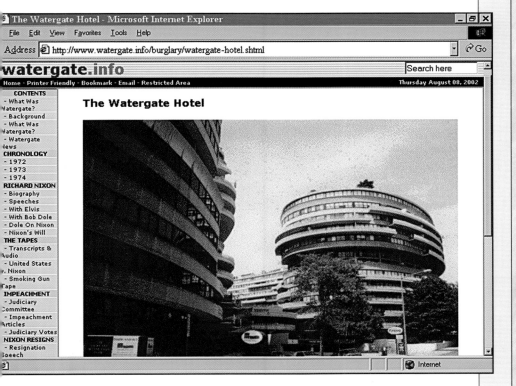

The Democratic National Committee offices located within the Watergate Hotel in Washington, D.C., were broken into on June 17, 1972.

Nixon. When this scandal erupted, it divided the nation and presented the most serious challenge to the U.S. Constitution of the twentieth century.

Each night on television, Americans could watch a real-life soap opera with the names, places, and events of the Watergate scandal. It would hold the public's interest for almost two years.

To fully understand what the Watergate scandal was, one has to go back to June 17, 1972. That is the date that a break-in at the Democratic Party headquarters in the Watergate building occurred.

That night, five burglars were captured in the offices of the Democratic National Committee. They were found carrying telephone wiretapping equipment and spy cameras.

One of the men captured was James W. McCord, Jr. He was a former Central Intelligence Agency (CIA) agent and security chief of the Committee to Re-elect the President (CREEP). John N. Mitchell, attorney general of the United States and chairman of CREEP, denied that his committee had anything to do with the burglary.

▶ Nixon Denies Any Involvement

Five days after the break-in, President Nixon stated in a press conference, "There is no involvement by the White House."[1] In addition, Nixon promised a full investigation into the case. In May 1973, Archibald Cox, a Harvard Law School professor, was named to head the investigation as the special prosecutor.

In November 1972, Nixon defeated George S. McGovern in the presidential election. The Republicans had collected a record sum for their campaign of over $60 million and ended with a surplus of more than $4 million.

From 1973 to 1974, investigations of the scandals developed and expanded. Many "White House horrors" dating back to President Nixon's first term were exposed. The term "White House horrors" itself was coined by Mitchell, who was also a former law partner of Nixon.[2] He used the term to describe the administration's secretive actions to ensure Nixon's reelection.

In the beginning, the American public regarded the Watergate scandal as nothing more than a problem with politics. Even in August 1972, after Washington newspapers had detailed how $114,000 in Nixon

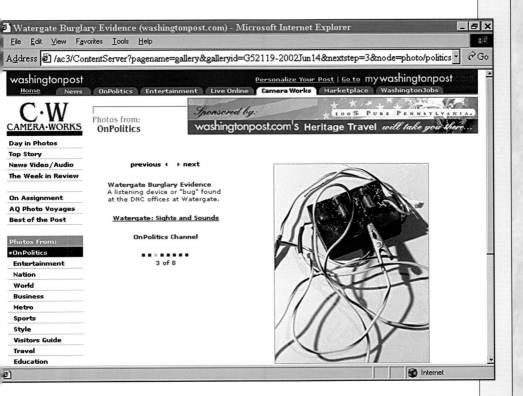

The information retrieved by listening devices planted in the Democratic National Committee offices, such as the one pictured here, was recorded by a receiver found at the Howard Johnson hotel across the street.

campaign checks had been deposited into the bank account of one of the burglars, the majority of the public still refused to believe that the president of the United States could have any involvement.

On September 15, 1972, the five burglars were indicted along with two other men: G. Gordon Liddy, an attorney for Nixon's campaign finance committee, and E. Howard Hunt, a former White House consultant and former CIA secret agent.

Early in 1973, evidence was presented that linked several top White House aides with either the break-in or later attempts to hide information related to it. Nixon continued to say that he did not know anything about that information. He kept promising that there would be a full investigation of the case.

▶ Nixon Refuses to Turn Over Tapes

In July, a Senate investigating committee learned that Nixon had secretly made tape recordings of conversations in his White House offices since 1971. Special prosecutor Archibald Cox and the committee asked the president for those tapes. The president refused, saying that the Constitution of the United States gave the president the implied right to keep his private conversations a secret.

Cox and the committee then filed petitions in court to obtain the tapes. U.S. District Court Judge John J. Sirica wanted to review the tapes himself. He ordered Nixon to turn over the tapes, and the president still declined.

In the meantime, Nixon offered to provide summaries of the tapes to the Senate committee. This time Cox refused, believing that they would not be regarded as proper evidence. Nixon then fired Cox.

Cox was later replaced by a noted Texas attorney, Leon Jaworski. These actions by Nixon resulted in the movement to begin the impeachment process.

Agnew Resigns

In August 1973, United States attorneys in Baltimore were investigating charges that Vice President Spiro Agnew had accepted bribes from contractors both before and after becoming vice president. Agnew denied the charges and even filed suit to try to stop the investigation.

On October 10, Agnew stunned the nation by announcing his resignation. He pleaded "no contest" to

▲ Many people poked fun at the Watergate scandal. This political cartoon refers to Richard Nixon's speech in which he declared that he was " . . . not a crook."

one charge of evading federal income taxes. Agnew was sentenced to three years probation and a $10,000 fine.

Just two days after Agnew's resignation, Nixon became the first president to nominate a vice president under the Twenty-Fifth Amendment to the Constitution. He nominated Gerald R. Ford, a Republican congressman from Michigan. Ford had also been minority leader in the House of Representatives since 1965.

Both houses of Congress confirmed the nomination, and Ford was sworn in as the country's fortieth vice president on December 6, 1973.

▶ Impeachment Hearings

In the winter of 1973–74, new events and revelations steadily worsened the president's position. He made unsuccessful efforts to regain public confidence by such measures as a television address on November 17, 1973, in which he declared, "I am not a crook."[3]

Impeachment hearings were held by the House Judiciary Committee in October 1973. Several times the committee attempted to obtain tapes of White House conversations through subpoenas. Each time Nixon refused.

With a huge television audience watching, the committee began public debate on articles of impeachment of the president on July 24, 1974. On July 27, the committee voted for impeachment of Nixon for obstructing justice in the Watergate cover-up. Two days later, the committee approved a second article of impeachment, charging the president with abuse of power and violation of the presidential oath of office.

A third article of impeachment for contempt of Congress was passed on July 30 because of Nixon's defiance of committee subpoenas.

Realizing that his impeachment would happen, Nixon released parts of the additional tapes he was required to turn over to the courts on August 5. It turned out to be the final straw for Nixon.

Almost all support for the president had now disappeared. On August 9, 1974, Richard Milhous Nixon became the first president ever to resign. In a televised speech to the nation the night before, the sixty-one-year-old Nixon explained his actions.

On the morning of August 9, Nixon and his wife, Pat, made an emotional farewell to his staff. They left the White House by helicopter, which flew them to Andrews Air Force Base. There they boarded *Air Force One* for their flight home to California.

The Nixons were going back to a private life.

On August 9, 1974, Richard Nixon became the first and only American president to ever resign from office. That morning he and Pat bid their farewell as they boarded the Marine One *helicopter.*

Chapter 2

Early Life, 1913–1945

Richard Milhous Nixon was born on January 9, 1913, on his parents' lemon farm in Yorba Linda, California. Yorba Linda is a village thirty miles southeast of Los Angeles.

Richard Nixon was the second of five sons born to Francis Anthony Nixon and Hannah Milhous Nixon. Those four brothers included one older one, Harold, and three younger ones, Donald, Arthur, and Edward.

Francis had moved to southern California from Ohio. Besides being a farmer, Francis also worked as a streetcar conductor, carpenter, and laborer.

It was there that he met and married Hannah Milhous. Hannah had come to California from Indiana with her parents and a group of other Quakers. Francis gave up his Methodist faith and became a Quaker when he wed Hannah.

Hannah was, as Richard later described her, "a gentle, Quaker mother, with a passionate concern for peace." She reared her five sons as Quakers and instilled in them the value of peace.[1]

In 1922, the Nixon family moved to Whittier, California, where his father opened a combination gasoline station and general store. It was in that store that the Nixon brothers worked when they were not in school.

By the time young Richard was ten, he began working as a part-time bean

◀ Richard Milhous Nixon, the second of five sons, was born at his parents' farm in Yorba Linda, California, on January 9, 1913.

Tools   Search   Notes   Discuss   Go!

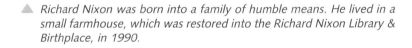

Birthplace – Microsoft Internet Explorer

File   Edit   View   Favorites   Tools   Help

Address   http://www.nixonfoundation.org/TheMuseum/Birthplace.shtml#P0_0   Go

THE RICHARD NIXON LIBRARY & BIRTHPLACE

debate RN's legacy 24-7 in the *NIXON FORUM*

[Hours & Directions]   [Contact Us]   [Search]

Buy Gifts, Books, Memorabilia & More in the **MUSEUM STORE**

SECRET TREATIES
Tools & Artifacts of Diplomacy

The Nixon Forum
Upcoming Events
Plan Your Event !
Museum Tour
Become A Member
Research Center
The Nixon Center
The Archives
Volunteer Opportunities

The Museum Tour

Birthplace

The Museum | The Birthplace | Permanent Galleries | Current Exhibits | Past Exhibits

On January 9, 1913, Richard Nixon was born in this little Yorba Linda Farmhouse. His father, Frank Nixon, built this house just a year earlier from a catalogue kit on 8.2 acres of our existing nine-acre museum site.

The Birthplace has been restored with attention to historical detail, on the exact spot where President Nixon's father built it. Although security and sprinkler systems have been installed, no part of the house was rebuilt. Most of the furnishings, including the bed where the President was born and the piano he learned to play are original.

Click Here to listen to the President describe his early life in Yorba Linda. Please be patient, as the sound file is large (1.45mb). A full text of the audio portion is available below.

http://discussion2.iland.com/~thenixonforum/   Internet

▲ *Richard Nixon was born into a family of humble means. He lived in a small farmhouse, which was restored into the Richard Nixon Library & Birthplace, in 1990.*

picker. As a teenager, Nixon worked as a handyman in a packinghouse, a janitor at a swimming pool, and a barker (someone who advertises by calling out to people) at an amusement park. When he was in college, Nixon was a bookkeeper and manager of the vegetable department of his father's store.

The Nixon family suffered two personal setbacks that would have deep impacts on Richard's life. The first came in 1925 when Richard's younger brother, Arthur, died from tuberculosis at the age of seven.

The second came seven years later when the eldest Nixon son, Harold, also died after a two-year battle with tuberculosis. Both deaths deeply affected Richard. He felt that it was his job to make up for both losses by becoming successful and sharing that success with his parents.[2]

▶ Nixon's Education

Nixon's elementary schooling took place in three cities— Yorba Linda, Whittier, and nearby Fullerton. Throughout his school career, Nixon took part in many activities and attained excellent grades. At Whittier High School, history and civics were Nixon's favorite subjects. That is where he played football and was a leading member of the debate team.

At seventeen, Nixon entered Whittier College, a Quaker institution. He had actually received a scholarship offer from Harvard University. Unfortunately, the scholarship only covered tuition. The Nixons did not have a lot of money, and young Richard could not afford any additional expenses for college. So he declined the offer from Harvard.

Instead, Nixon continued to be active at Whittier College. He continued his work on the debate team and won prizes for public speaking. He also acted in plays, performed on the organ at the Quaker meeting house, and played the piano at parties.

It was while at Whittier that Nixon became involved in politics and was elected to several school offices. That included being elected president of the college student body. When he graduated from Whittier College in 1934, Nixon was second in his class.

Nixon's education did not end with Whittier. He won a tuition scholarship from the Duke University School of Law in Durham, North Carolina. Unlike his situation with Harvard, Nixon accepted this offer. He was able to pay for the rest of his expenses by doing research for the dean for thirty-five cents an hour.

While at Duke, Nixon was elected president of the student law association. He also won election to the Order of the Coif, the national law fraternity for honor students. When he graduated from Duke in 1937, Nixon ranked third in his class of forty-four students.

▶ Nixon as a Lawyer and Family Man

Jobs were hard to find during the Great Depression. Nixon attempted to land a job with the FBI, but he was unsuccessful. It was the same story when he applied to a law firm in New York City.

Nixon decided to return to California. He took the state bar examination, passed it, and joined a law firm in Whittier, where he became a partner. Nixon was appointed as a member of the Whittier College Board of Trustees. At twenty-six, he was the youngest member of the board.

▲ Richard and Pat Nixon had two daughters. Seated from left to right are David Eisenhower, (husband to Nixon's youngest daughter, Julie) Julie Nixon Eisenhower, Richard, Pat, and Tricia Nixon.

During this same period of time, Nixon joined a local amateur theater group. It was there he met Thelma Catherine "Pat" Ryan, a high school teacher.

Ryan was born in a mining camp at Ely, Nevada. She was nicknamed Pat by her father because she was born on the eve of St. Patrick's Day. The Ryans moved to California when Pat was just a baby. Unfortunately, her parents died before she finished high school. The tragedy did not stop Pat from achieving her goals. She put herself through school at the University of Southern California.

Nixon proposed marriage to Pat the night they met. After refusing him for two years, she finally married him on June 21, 1940. The couple would have two daughters, Patricia (Tricia), born in 1946, and Julie, born in 1948. Julie later married David Eisenhower, grandson of former President Dwight D. Eisenhower, in 1968. Tricia would marry Edward Cox in 1971.

▶ Nixon Joins the Navy

In January 1942, Nixon left Whittier and headed to Washington, D.C. Once in Washington, Nixon took a $61-a-week job in the tire rationing section of the Office of Price Administration.

Eight months later, Nixon decided to join the Navy, despite his peaceful Quaker background. In September 1942, Nixon applied for, and received, a navy commission as a lieutenant j.g. (junior grade). In 1943, he was sent to the South Pacific as operations officer for a navy air transport unit.

After fifteen months, Nixon returned to shore duty in the United States. By the time the war ended in 1945, he had advanced to the rank of lieutenant commander.

Chapter 3 ▶

Congressman to Senator, 1945–1952

In November 1945, Richard Nixon was awaiting his release from the Navy. Friends of his began to suggest that he consider entering politics. The suggestion was that Nixon run for Congress in the 1946 election. It did not take long for the naval officer to make up his mind.

The idea was to have the Republican Committee back Nixon to run against Democratic candidate Jerry Voorhis, for the U.S. House of Representatives. Voorhis had been the Democratic representative from California's Twelfth District for ten years.

Nixon campaigned aggressively, using tactics that he would become famous for later in his political career. Nixon accused Voorhis of being a Communist, although there was no real proof that he was. The Republican candidate also ridiculed his opponent's past record in Congress. Voorhis tried to attack Nixon, but since Nixon had no prior political record, Voorhis was forced to defend himself. The thirty-three-year-old Nixon won the election and was on his way to Washington.

▶ Nixon the Congressman

Nixon became one of the youngest members of the Republican-controlled Eightieth Congress, which President Harry Truman came to label as the "Do-Nothing Congress."[1]

One of the first committees that Nixon was assigned to was the Education and Labor Committee. It was there that Nixon was introduced to another freshman congressman,

John F. Kennedy. The two would continue to cross paths over the next fourteen years.

One of the major efforts of the committee was to write the Taft-Hartley Act, called the "slave labor law" by unions. This act established controls over the unions.

It should also be noted that between 1947 and 1948 the Cold War was developing between the United States and the Soviet Union. It was becoming quite apparent to the United States that Russia was not going to let the countries of Eastern Europe that it had "liberated" during World War II choose their own governments.[2] Nixon's outspoken views against Communism would influence his involvement with two other committees he would be appointed to.

One of those committees he was named to was the Herter Committee, which helped lay the groundwork for the Marshall Plan and other foreign-aid programs. On a trip to

Nixon was the underdog in the California congressional election of 1946. Shown here is an ad campaign he used to secure victory.

Europe with other members of the committee, Nixon learned that to prevent war-torn countries in Western Europe from falling into the hands of Communists, they would need economic or foreign aid. When Nixon returned to the United States, he became a strong supporter of foreign aid.

Nixon Makes a Name for Himself

Nixon was also assigned to the House Un-American Activities Committee. It was a prestigious post for the young congressman. The committee was established to see the extent of Communist influence on the United States government, the motion-picture industry, and other areas of American life.

In 1948, Nixon won reelection to the House for two more years. That same year, the Alger Hiss case gained national attention. This would bring Nixon popularity across the country. Hiss was a former State Department official. He was accused of having given classified State Department documents to a Soviet spy ring during the 1930s.

Following a great deal of questioning by the House Un-American Activities Committee, it came down to Hiss's word against that of his accusers. Several members of the committee wanted to drop the case.

Nixon was against dropping it. He insisted that the charges against Hiss be either proved or disproved.

Following months of further investigation and questioning, a New York grand jury indicted Hiss for perjury. That trial ended in a hung jury in July 1949. There was a retrial, and in January 1950, Hiss was found guilty and sentenced to five years in prison.

Nixon Becomes a Senator

Riding on the success he had achieved as a Communist hunter, Nixon decided to run for the United States Senate in 1950. He ran against Democratic Congresswoman Helen Gahagan Douglas.

Once again, Nixon went on the offensive in his campaign, attacking Douglas's reputation. Nixon claimed that she had supported Communist policy against the best interests of the United States, calling her the "Pink Lady."[3] Any ties between Douglas and Communism were never proven.

Later, Douglas would label Nixon as "Tricky Dick," a nickname that would remain with him the rest of his life.[4]

In the end, Nixon won the election by nearly seven hundred thousand votes, becoming, at thirty-seven, the youngest Republican U.S. senator.

The freshman senator joined a Senate that was controlled by Democrats. Because of that, Nixon was given few significant assignments. He served on the Labor and Public Welfare Committee. Nixon also became a popular public speaker, speaking at Republican Party affairs and civic meetings across the United States.

Ironically, it was while on a trip to Europe that he met with General Dwight D. Eisenhower. At the time, Eisenhower was being urged to run for president.

After meeting the general, Nixon joined the Eisenhower campaign for the Republican presidential nomination.

It was a move that would have a major impact on the next part of Nixon's political life.

General Dwight D. Eisenhower chose Nixon to be his running mate for the 1952 presidential election.

Chapter 4 ▶

Vice President to Early Retirement, 1952–1962

"No one has done more to put the fear of God into those who would betray their country."[1]

That is what one of the speakers who supported Richard Nixon's candidacy for vice president had to say at the Republican National Convention in July 1952, in Chicago, Illinois.

Nominating Dwight Eisenhower as their presidential candidate was easy. Eisenhower then invited Nixon to be his vice-presidential running mate. However, by the time September rolled around it looked as though Nixon may have to drop out of the race. The *New York Post* newspaper had run a story accusing Nixon of using a secret $18,000 fund collected by a "millionaires' club" for personal expenses.[2]

▶ Checkers Speech

Eisenhower was under pressure to remove Nixon from the ticket, but he refused. On September 23, five days after the story had broken, Nixon, with his wife at his side, appeared on a national television show to clarify the issue. Sixty million people watched and listened as Nixon explained that the fund had been used solely to aid his political campaign and had not been used for personal expenses.[3] Nixon concluded his remarks with a story about a dog:

> We did get something—a gift—after the election [for senator].
> A man down in Texas heard Pat mention on the radio the fact
> that our two youngsters would like to have a dog. And believe
> it or not, the day before we left on this campaign trip we got a

▲ Nixon served as vice president under President Dwight D. Eisenhower from 1952 to 1960.

message from Union Station in Baltimore saying they had a package for us. We went down to get it. You know what it was? It was a little cocker spaniel dog in a crate that he sent all the way from Texas. Black-and-white spotted. And our little girl—Tricia, the six year old—named it Checkers. And you know, the kids love that dog and I just want to say right now that, regardless of what 'they' say about it, we're going to keep it.[4]

Thus, the "Checkers" speech was born. In the closing moments of the speech Nixon assured the viewers that he "was not a quitter." He finally told the viewing audience to send in their views as to what he should do.

Over the next few days, millions of calls and letters came in from all over the United States in support of Nixon and his touching story about Checkers the dog. The

Eisenhower-Nixon ticket won the 1952 election by a landslide, something they would do again in 1956.

Active Vice President

Eisenhower gave Nixon the responsibility of working with members of Congress to smooth out possible quarrels with the new administration. The new president also assigned his vice president to preside over Cabinet meetings and the National Security Council in Eisenhower's absence. It was obvious that Nixon was taking a more active role in the government than many previous vice presidents.

Nixon's greatest challenge as vice president came on September 24, 1955, when Eisenhower suffered a heart attack. Nixon showed his true leadership qualities by going

▲ The televised debates between Nixon and John F. Kennedy aided the outcome of the 1960 presidential election.

about the president's normal duties, keeping the wheels of government moving smoothly.

Nixon would again step in for the president when Eisenhower was bothered by an intestinal disorder in 1956 and a stroke in 1957. Each time, the vice president kept the executive branch of the government moving right along.

Nixon on Foreign Affairs

Nixon was frequently asked by Eisenhower to represent him as a spokesperson for the United States on goodwill trips to foreign countries. Over the course of eight years as vice president, Nixon visited fifty-four nations.

In the spring of 1958, Nixon made a visit to Latin America. He faced violence and danger almost the entire time he was there. Communist agents led groups in Peru that booed and threw rocks at Nixon. In Venezuela, mobs broke the windows on Nixon's car, although the vice president was not hurt.

In July 1959, Nixon traveled to the Soviet Union to open an American exhibit in Moscow. As he and Soviet Premier Nikita S. Khrushchev walked through the exhibit, they continually argued over which economic system was better—capitalism or communism. By the time they got to the model of the modern American home, they were standing in the kitchen verbally battling it out. Most observers on hand that day felt that Nixon had come out ahead.

Nixon Runs for President

By the end of 1959, there was no doubt in anyone's mind that Nixon would be the Republican candidate for the next presidential election. The only opposition came from Nelson Rockefeller, the governor of New York.

By the time the Republican National Convention was held in Chicago in July 1960, Nixon was nominated on the first ballot. Nixon then chose Henry Cabot Lodge, Jr., U.S. ambassador to the United Nations, as his vice-presidential running mate.

The Democrats nominated Senator John F. Kennedy, Jr., of Massachusetts for president and Senator Lyndon B. Johnson, of Texas, as vice president.

Nixon reluctantly agreed to do a series of four televised debates with Kennedy.

The debates made a huge difference and turned out to be the downfall for Nixon. In the first debate on television, Kennedy wore makeup and looked tanned and relaxed. Nixon, on the other hand, refused makeup and looked white and pasty, almost sickly.

Nixon's own mother phoned him following the first debate to ask her son if "he was feeling all right."[5]

Nixon lost to Kennedy in one of the closest presidential elections in United States history. Of the nearly 69 million votes cast, Kennedy won by 118,574 popular votes. While Nixon may have carried 26 states to 22 for

Many believed that Richard Nixon's political career was over after he lost both the presidential elections of 1960 and the California gubernatorial race in 1962.

Kennedy, the Democratic candidate received 303 electoral votes to 219 for Nixon.

There were some at the time who also felt that there was fraud in the vote count in Texas and Illinois, both of which went to Kennedy by small margins. They wanted a recount of votes, but Nixon was against the idea. Nixon conceded the election to Kennedy.

▶ Nixon Runs for Governor

With his term as vice president completed, Nixon returned to California. There he joined a law firm in Los Angeles. In 1961, he wrote the book *Six Crises,* which highlighted his career. It was published in 1962.

That same year, Nixon announced that he would run for governor of California against Democratic Governor Edmund G. "Pat" Brown. Brown easily defeated Nixon, winning with 53.6 percent of the vote.

Two major political defeats within two years was more than Nixon could deal with. At a press conference held shortly after his defeat to Brown, Nixon said, ". . . as I leave you I want you to know—just think how much you're going to be missing. You won't have Nixon to kick around anymore, because, gentlemen, this is my last press conference . . . Thank you gentlemen and good day."[6]

Most people that day believed that Nixon's political career was over.

Chapter 5

Becoming President Nixon, 1963–1973

If anyone thought that Nixon was finished with politics in 1962, they were quite mistaken. In 1963, Nixon moved back east to New York City. There he took a well-paid job with a large law firm called Mudge, Rose, Guthrie, & Alexander.

▶ Nixon Back on the Campaign Trail

Nixon had supporters who wanted him to run for president in 1964. He declined. However, beginning in 1965,

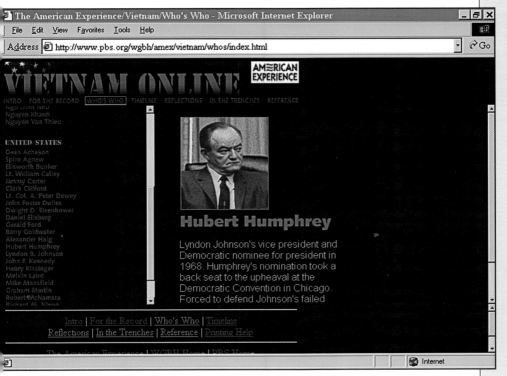

▲ Both Richard Nixon and Hubert Humphrey promised an end to the Vietnam War during the 1968 presidential election.

Nixon went back on the campaign trail. The former vice president campaigned vigorously for Republican candidates throughout the United States in the elections of 1965 and 1966.

By 1967, Nixon was traveling around the world, including visits to South Vietnam and the Soviet Union. Before the end of the year, Nixon was a leading contender for the presidency. By November 1967, opinion polls indicated that Nixon was more popular than President Johnson.

In February 1968, Nixon announced that he was a candidate for the Republican presidential nomination. Following another hard campaign, Nixon was once again nominated on the first ballot at the Republican National Convention held that summer in Miami, Florida. His choice for vice-presidential running mate would be Maryland Governor Spiro Agnew.

The Nixon-Agnew duo would run against Democratic Vice President Hubert H. Humphrey and his running mate, Senator Edmund Muskie of Maine. There was also a

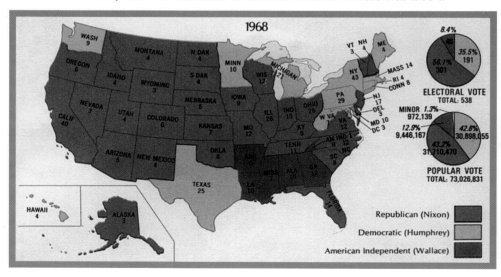

▲ *A map of the presidential election of 1968.*

third party running that year, the American Independent Party. Its candidate for president was George C. Wallace, the former governor of Alabama. His running mate was retired Air Force General Curtis LeMay.

The Vietnam War was the main issue of the campaign, with both Nixon and Humphrey promising to bring an end to the war.

In the election, Nixon beat Humphrey by only approximately 511,000 popular votes, 31,785,480 to 31,275,166. Wallace received 9,906,473 popular votes. Nixon was the electoral votes winner, capturing 301. Humphrey was second with 191 and Wallace a distant third with 46.

Nixon became the highest-paid president at the time. Less than a week before he was inaugurated as the nation's thirty-seventh president, Congress doubled the presidential salary from $100,000 to $200,000.

▶ Foreign Policy

One goal that Nixon had set for himself was a settlement of the war in Vietnam. The Vietnam peace talks, which had started in 1968, continued in 1969, but with little progress. In March 1969, Nixon presented a policy known as "Vietnamization." This continued the training program for South Vietnamese forces so they could eventually take over the major part of the fighting.

The United States involvement in the war continued over the next three years. In 1972, Nixon ordered a blockade of North Vietnam to cut off war supplies from China and the Soviet Union. Late in the year, Nixon ordered more bombing of Hanoi, the capital of North Vietnam.

Nixon Visits China and Soviet Union

Nixon improved relations with China and the Soviet Union. In 1969, the president approved the removal of travel restrictions on Americans wanting to go to China. He also encouraged the reopening of trade between the two countries. In February 1972, Nixon visited China, himself.

Three months later, Nixon traveled to the Soviet Union. He signed agreements with Leonid I. Brezhnev, leader of the Soviet Union, to limit production of nuclear weapons. Later in the year, the Soviet Union became a major buyer of wheat from the United States.

Nixon on the Home Front

The new president was also accomplishing a great deal on the national scene. In 1969, Congress passed Nixon's proposal to

The Vietnam War was extremely controversial. Many people, such as those shown here, protested American involvement. In response, President Nixon proposed his policy of "Vietnamization."

establish a lottery system for the military draft. Later that year, Congress approved extensive reforms in federal tax laws.

In March 1969, Nixon proposed a plan to build an antiballistic missile (ABM) system called Safeguard. The president felt that new missiles were needed to protect United States underground missiles and bomber bases from enemy attack. Following several months of debate, the Senate approved the construction of two such ABM bases.

One of the most monumental moments in Nixon's first administration came on July 20, 1969. That was the date on which *Apollo 11* astronauts Neil A. Armstrong and Edwin E. "Buzz" Aldrin, Jr., became the first people to set foot on the moon.

Back here on earth, environmental problems were beginning to endanger many aspects of life in the United States. In 1970, Nixon set up the Environmental Protection Agency to deal with the pollution problems.

In 1970, Congress lowered the minimum voting age in federal elections from twenty-one to eighteen. This was accomplished through the Twenty-Sixth Amendment to the U.S. Constitution, which was ratified in 1971.

Nixon's revenue sharing program was also passed by Congress in 1972. This gave tax money back to state and local governments.

▶ Nixon's Second Term

The American public seemed pleased with the progress the Nixon administration made in its first four years. It came as no surprise when Nixon and Agnew easily won the 1972 presidential election, defeating the Democratic Party's presidential candidate, Senator George S. McGovern from South Dakota, and his running mate, Sargent Shriver, former director of the Peace Corps.

Nixon received almost 18 million more popular votes than McGovern. Nixon also got 520 electoral votes to McGovern's 17.

Economic Crisis

The Nixon administration had to deal with economic problems on the home front in his first term in office. Those problems did not go away as he entered his second term.

End of United States Involvement in Vietnam War

Nixon hoped that peace talks between the United States and North Vietnam would go smoothly after his second

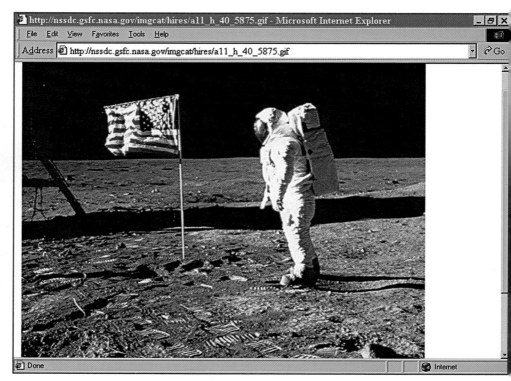

Buzz Aldrin was one of the first people to walk on the moon.

election to office. Unfortunately, that did not happen, and talks broke off in mid-December 1972.

On December 18, Nixon ordered the heaviest bombing attacks ever against North Vietnam. On December 30, Nixon announced that the bombing would stop and peace negotiations would resume in Paris.

On January 15, Nixon stopped all bombing on North Vietnam. Five days later, in his second inaugural address, the president said: "We stand on the threshold of a new era of peace in the world."[1]

On January 27, 1973, the United States and other participants in the Vietnam War signed agreements to stop fighting immediately. An exchange of prisoners began as well. A great deal of credit is given to Henry A. Kissinger, Nixon's chief foreign-policy adviser. Later that year, Kissinger became secretary of state.

The United States completed its troop withdrawal from South Vietnam in March. Things looked good for the United States and the Nixon administration. A new era of peace had begun.

Before Americans could begin to enjoy this new peace, however, a new crisis was stirring. Criticism of the Watergate scandal would intensify in the coming months.

Chapter 6

Elder Statesman,
1974–1994

At 12:01 P.M. on August 9, 1974, Richard Nixon officially resigned as president of the United States.

On that day he and his wife, Pat, boarded *Marine One,* the president's official helicopter, on the grounds of the White House. Moments later the helicopter lifted off and flew to Andrews Air Force Base. There, the Nixons boarded *Air Force One* for their flight home to San Clemente, California.

Despite his resignation, there were still many Americans who continued to debate whether Nixon should be brought to trial for his cover-up of the Watergate scandal.

Nixon himself was very depressed and seemed to be in deep despair during his first weeks back in California. The cloud of Watergate hung over Nixon's head and would not go away.

▶ Nixon Given Pardon

On September 8, 1974, President Gerald Ford granted Nixon a "full, free, and absolute" pardon for all federal crimes Nixon may have committed while in office. It was a move that surprised and shocked the nation. With this action, Ford kept Nixon from the possibility of criminal indictment and a trial.

In accepting the pardon, Nixon again made no admission of guilt. He said:

> No words can describe the depths of my regret and pain at the anguish my mistakes over Watergate have caused the nation and the Presidency, a nation I so deeply love and an

institution I so greatly respect. I know that many fair-minded people believe that my motivation and actions in the Watergate affair were intentionally self-serving and illegal. I now understand how my own mistakes and misjudgments have contributed to that belief and seemed to support it. This burden is the heaviest one of all to bear.[1]

▶ Nixon Close to Death

The mental strain that Nixon was suffering at the time was being equally matched by physical problems. Nixon's leg swelled up with phlebitis (an inflamed vein), when a large and life-threatening blood clot formed.

On October 30, 1974, Nixon went through a seventy-minute operation to correct the problem. Following a

▲ President Gerald Ford's pardon of Nixon for any crimes he might have committed while in office was very controversial. Many believed that the former president should have been brought to trial.

setback after the operation that nearly killed him, Nixon eventually recovered after several months of rehabilitation.

▶ Author

Four years later, in 1978, Nixon published his autobiography, *RN: The Memoirs of Richard Nixon.* In the book, he admitted involvement in the efforts to cover up White House participation in the Watergate affair. He disclosed that he preserved the tapes that were ultimately his undoing, because he believed they would protect him from charges by aides who might testify against him.[2]

It seemed to be the jump-start Nixon needed to begin his comeback with the American public.

In 1980, Richard and Pat Nixon moved back east to New York City to be closer to the rest of his family, which now included grandchildren. Nixon would also be closer to the central parts of political power based out of Washington, D.C.

That same year he published *The Real War,* a book based on United States foreign policy during the Cold War.

In 1981, the Nixons moved again, this time to Saddle River, New Jersey. He continued to author several more books, including *Leaders* in 1982; *Real Peace: A Strategy for the West* in 1983; *No More Vietnams,* 1985; *In the Arena,* 1990; and *Beyond Peace* in 1994.

Ten years after his resignation, Nixon had transformed his status from being a bitter exile to being an influential ex-president. To his delight, even the *New York Times* acknowledged this transformation in a graceful tribute by John Herbers:

"A decade later he has emerged at seventy-one years of age as an elder statesman, commentator on foreign and domestic affairs, adviser to world leaders, a multi-millionaire and a successful author and lecturer honored by audiences at home and abroad."[3]

Nixon continued his world travels. These included trips to meet with major political leaders in China and the Soviet Union. Both countries welcomed him with open arms.

The former president was even invited back to the White House to discuss world problems with fellow-Republican Presidents Ronald Reagan and George H. W. Bush.

If there was a defining moment when Nixon finally gained some acceptance and forgiveness by the American public it came in April 1986. That is when the magazine *Newsweek* ran a cover story using the headline, "He's Back: The Rehabilitation of Richard Nixon."

▲ Even after an embarrassing leave of office, Richard Nixon was still an influential voice in politics. Here he is gathered with presidents Ronald Reagan, George H. W. Bush, and Gerald Ford in July 1990 to dedicate the Richard Nixon Library & Birthplace.

Final Years

In 1990, the Richard Nixon Library and Birthplace, which also includes a museum, was dedicated and opened in Yorba Linda. It was one of the proudest moments in Nixon's career.

The following year the Nixons were on the move again, this time moving to Park Ridge, New Jersey.

Unfortunately, Pat, the love of Nixon's life for over fifty years, developed lung cancer. On June 22, 1993, the former first lady died at their home in Park Ridge.

Despite his loss, Nixon continued on with his life, busier than ever. Then, ten months after Pat's death, Richard Nixon suffered a massive stroke on April 18, 1994, while having dinner at home.

Three days later, Nixon fell into a coma. On April 22, Nixon died. He was buried next to his wife, Pat, on the grounds of the Richard Nixon Library and Birthplace in Yorba Linda.

Nixon Remembered

There are many mixed reviews of Richard Nixon and his presidency. On one hand, he is remembered as the first president to resign to avoid

Although Richard Nixon accomplished many things during his two terms as president, he may be best remembered for his role in covering up the Watergate scandal.

impeachment and conviction by Congress for misuse of power.

Ironically, his two terms as chief executive were equally split. In his first term, from 1969 to 1973, the Nixon Administration is remembered for its achievements in foreign policy. Especially the improved relations with Russia and China.

Nixon also helped end the United States involvement in the unpopular Vietnam War, the longest and one of the costliest wars in United States history. Still, his second term was wrecked by the Watergate scandals, and this is what people seem to remember most. A poll conducted by the Federalist Society and the *Wall Street Journal* in 2000, ranked Nixon in the "below average" category, thirty-third of the thirty-nine presidents that were graded. When Jimmy Carter was governor of Georgia, he once said of Nixon, "in two hundred years of history, he's the most dishonest president we've ever had."[4]

Author Jonathan Aitken, who wrote *Nixon: A Life*, summed up how Nixon would like to be remembered in the epilogue of his book:

> There is a growing willingness to accept that his achievements as a peacemaker and international statesman give him a strong claim to be regarded as America's finest foreign policy president of the twentieth century. If he eventually achieves that historical honor, alongside the contemporary dishonor of being the first and only president to resign, the scales of judgement will at last be more evenly balanced.[5]

Chapter Notes

Chapter 1. The Watergate Scandal, 1973–1974

1. David C. Whitney, *The American Presidents* (Garden City, N.Y.: Doubleday & Company, 2001), p. 353.

2. Ibid., p. 352.

3. Ibid., p. 360.

Chapter 2. Early Life, 1913–1945

1. David C. Whitney, *The American Presidents* (Garden City, N.Y.: Doubleday & Company, 2001), p. 330.

2. *Richard Nixon, Man and President*, A&E Biography. New Video Group, 1996, videocassette.

Chapter 3. Congressman to Senator, 1945–1952

1. David C. Whitney, *The American Presidents* (Garden City, N.Y.: Doubleday & Company, 2001), p. 331.

2. Ibid., p. 332.

3. *Richard Nixon, Man and President*, A&E Biography. New Video Group, 1996, videocassette.

4. Ibid.

Chapter 4. Vice President to Early Retirement, 1952–1962

1. David C. Whitney, *The American Presidents* (Garden City, N.Y.: Doubleday & Company, Inc., 2001), p. 334.

2. Ibid.

3. Ibid.

4. Jonathan Aitken, *Nixon: A Life* (D.C.: Regnery Publishing, Inc., 1996), pp. 216–217.

5. *Richard Nixon, Man and President*, A&E Biography. New Video Group, 1996, videocassette.

6. Ibid., p. 305.

Chapter 5. Becoming President Nixon, 1963–1973

1. Richard M. Nixon, "Second Inaugural Address," reprinted on *Bartleby.com*, 2003, <http://www.bartleby.com/124/pres59.html> (January 23, 2003).

Chapter 6. Elder Statesman, 1974–1994

1. David C. Whitney, *The American Presidents* (Garden City, N.Y.: Doubleday & Company, Inc., 2001), p. 363.

2. Ibid.

3. Jonathan Aitken, *Nixon: A Life* (D.C.: Regnery Publishing, Inc., 1996), p. 560.

4. Jimmy Carter, as quoted in William A. DeGregorio, *The Complete Book of U.S. Presidents: From George Washington to Bill Clinton* (New York: Wings Books, 1997), p. 600.

5. Aitken, p. 560.

Further Reading

Barron, Rachel Stiffler. *Richard Nixon: American Politician.* Greensboro, N.C.: Reynolds, Morgan Inc, 1998.

Cohen, Daniel. *Watergate: Deception in the White House.* Brookfield, Conn.: Millbrook Press, Inc., 1998.

Gaines, Ann Graham. *Richard M. Nixon: Our Thirty-Seventh President.* Chanhassen, Minn.: The Child's World, Inc., 2001.

Genovese, Michael A. *The Watergate Crisis.* Westport, Conn.: Greenwood Publishing Group, Inc., 1999.

Green, Robert. *Richard M. Nixon.* Minneapolis, Minn.: Compass Point Books, 2003.

Herda, D. J. *United States vs. Nixon: Watergate and the President.* Springfield, N.J.: Enslow Publishers, Inc., 1996.

Joes, Anthony James. *The War for South Vietnam, 1954–1975.* Revised Edition. Westport, Conn.: Greenwood Publishing Group, Inc., 2001.

Kilian, Pamela. *What Was Watergate?* New York: Saint Martin's Press, LLC, 1990.

Lucas, Eileen. *Nixon, Ford, and Carter.* Vero Beach, Fla.: Rourke Corporation, 1996.

Nadel, Laurie. *The Great Stream of History: A Biography of Richard M. Nixon.* New York: Atheneum Books for Young Readers, 1991.

Stefoff, Rebecca and Richard G. Young, ed. *Richard M. Nixon: Thirty-Seventh President of the United States.* Ada, Okla.: Garrett Educational Corporation, 1990.

Index